Loss X Mental Illness

Aariona Harris

Publisher Contact: prolificpulse.com

ISBN: Paperback ISBN: 978-1-962374-10-1

ISBN: ePub 978-1-962374-11-8

Library of Congress Control Number: 2024901891

Permissions have been granted and filed by the
publisher.
Publisher: Prolific Pulse Press LLC
Prolificpulse.com

Cover Design: Kelli R. Jackson

Published February 2024, Raleigh, North Carolina
USA

Table Of Contents

Dedication

For those of us who know what it's like to move forward without a loved one, and those of us who do it while facing other internal challenges. For my mom, Ratanya Harris. I didn't tell you I love you enough when you were here. I'm making up for that, it's eternal now. Inked out in black and printed on white pages.

Acknowledgments

"Growing Up," "Vacation," "Worn Book Pages," "Guilty Conscious," and "Empath" were published by *Lothlorien Poetry Journal,* 2023.

"Vacation" *was published by Fine Lines Literary Journal,* 2023.

"Un-Made" and "You" have been published in *Prolific Pulsations anthology,* 2023.

Drowning; Deep Water

I have loved and lost

Forced to pay such a cost

My heart has splintered

Hands turned to stone

I now live in a world

In which you are gone

A disastrous punishment

One I did not earn

I'll pull it together for you.

Claw my way from deep

below the earth, be the daughter

you've always known I could be

the one you deserved.

LIFE

You ever wonder what the meaning of life is?

Is it like this- a flash in the abyss?

No one knows why we do it or what the result will be.

We all have our own ideas, thoughts and wishes.

Hopeless.

But we won't stop, like a piece of plastic drifting aimlessly

or a seashell being washed back to sea

live my life and give my life

in the name of the country who saves

but are we all simply graves?

Does it end with a flash in the abyss?

Chemical Imbalances

Embrace the meaning of forever

hold on to your ideas of together

go tell your feeble heart to hush

tangible thoughts of smelling the rose bush

give it your all, fall

hopelessly dangerously and unequivocally

in love with finding the words to

define love.

Ever Changing Skies

People drift away

leave their mark, though none will stay

we all tell a story, mine is

certainly, a cause for worry.

How do you survive in a world

meant for your demise?

How to live when you've given

all you have and can find?

Lose your soul

but reach your goal

no one is in your corner

no one is on your team

it is all going to be alright

it is all going to be okay

hold your head high

smile and wave.

People drift away but

they say we'll always make it through the day.

Anxiety

My personal hell

no way to bail

yet these prisoners

lead me to fail

breathe

we feel, but don't

the monster wont

let us

breathe

Numbing the pain

no personal gain

we try in vain

to breathe

a vice like grip

on these lips.

I can't speak.

I can't leave.

I can't breathe.

Musical Rescue

Almost my saviors

the artists do me a favor

their music delivers

a soft caress, a shiver

a new feeling

brings to me a way to forget

this reeling

one song replaces endless regret

the things we all want to forget

Worn Book Pages

I've lived so many lives in just this one

I know my time on this earth isn't done

somehow I've aged beyond these 23 years

yet still, I have not conquered any of my fears

Today, I am as old as the earth

i molded into the dirt and listened to its stories

i sway in the wind like a great oak tree

together we screech through the night

and hope that my old and tired body is not yet done

putting up a fight.

because life is pain, and death nothingness

but I refuse to go quietly into the night.

Panic

I forgot how to breathe

catastrophic events behind

these eyes; distracted me

abandoned train tracks

i'm in need of repair

of a way

to give this pain back

my mind is a fighting machine

throwing sharp knives dipped in poison

shooting bullets filled with disease at me

I've not learned to be brave

not in the face of the monster

I call a brain

if only they knew

if only they could see

these events have blinded me.

and I seem to have

forgotten how to breathe.

Drifting Away

On these days I'm proud and I cry

for progress and healing

because I've come to be friends

friendly, with my grief.

Blossoming in its darkness

we've come to an understanding.

On days when I'm not so sad

I fear my friend will fade away

leaving behind old memories I've shelved

building dust like an unattended library

too brittle to remain whole

I worry that thoughts of my lost ones

will cease playing on repeat in my head.

I dread over the possibility that one day

I'll forget the smallest of details

on these days when I'm not so sad

I am terrified.

Manic Possibilities

Today my mind isn't screaming at me in anger

it doesn't feel some sense of danger

this day feels different

I wonder why

Is this a turning point?

Am I done bleeding myself dry?

No one has all of the answers

and even if it's fleeting

this feeling I'm receiving

I'll embrace it and

pray there comes no harm

hold myself together until the dawn

of another day as 24 hours washes away

I'll be left to remember

I've been happy on this day.

You

I am you

in the way that I love

your favorite song

I'm a combination of your thoughts

every part of me was made from you

every part of you holds some truth

some secret facet of information

which holds in each piece

a sliver of my salvation

I am you

and you are me

Empath

Do you ever know something which you cannot know?

See the truth of a thing

though no one has informed you.

Have to take a moment to not feel every feeling?

Not feel-the unconscious need to be understood

I know these feelings intimately

yet they are not my own

this burden does not leave me

does not vacate the premises of my soul

though it senses the havoc which has been reaped.

I understand the lives of others

I see their brokenness

have made a family with their darkness

I do not wish to know things, I'll forget what I know about
me.

So I listen to the darkness and wait in fear.

Wondering if it might extend to me-

one last request.

Quiet these souls

and reveal nothing else.

Wonder

I wonder about the world

the intimate workings of it

The fairness or indifference

the vastness of this universe

I wonder about our lives

how miniscule and insignificant

how uninvolved and moot

how desperate we are to survive

I can't help but wonder about love, a space where
our souls are protected

a promise of unconditional understanding

I wonder about the devastation of loss

what it means to love someone and lose them

what to do about the world continuing

what to see as it turns

when all you wish is for it to burn.

Fallacies

I believe

in lies and falsehoods

crave the safety of fallacy

obsess over the freedom in faith

want to be unabridged from the truth

fiction is a mix of beauty and magic

ethereal protection from reality

lies free me

from the danger of what is real

and lock me in a cocoon of safety

which in reality is insanity

I believe in the generosity

of deceit.

Writer's Block

I cannot discern these thoughts I hold captive

they rattle around my empty skull

fighting to latch onto one another

in hopes that they might form

one coherent idea

one creative word

yet it is an upward battle

one in which they should not hope to win

because I cannot discern these thoughts

nor this havoc that has been wrought

and therefore I have nothing

no thoughts

to give.

Absence

I am lost without you

making attempts to perfect my role

in this world Empty of your soul

I must go on, move forward toward my destiny

attempt to remember what it was like

to live in a place free of this agony

in the silence filled with my screams

I ask myself, is survival guaranteed?

If I cannot project regality, behave as a queen

disguise this pain beneath a crown,

however will I survive

and not crumble to the ground?

Un-Made

I wish to disappear

to erase my essence, as though I were never here

I crave the knowledge of nonexistence

to vanquish my involvement in this.

Dive into an abyss and drown there for an eternity

unfeeling and disconnected, even from my family

oblivious to the chaos that is the world

ignorant of the biases which make it whirl

utterly unburdened and in bliss.

I can taste the freedom of this

and I cannot help but wish.

Victimless Crime

For your loss

they say I'm sorry

they offer condolences

as swiftly as apologies

they bring by meals

and bake extra pies

filling our heads and ears

with their consistent lies

of a better time to come

but there is no escape

from these truths which

they so vehemently shove in our face

we have been a victim

of Fate

Hi, it's nice to meet you

We're acquaintances, my depression and I

much like the coworkers you have drinks with

you don't exactly like them

but you're stuck in a very particular hell

and so, you're in this together

My depression reminds me of things

I might otherwise have the pleasure of forgetting

'Don't forget you've suffered great loss!'

'Try not to think so hard about being alone!'

Nothing helpful, reminders, nonetheless.

I've come to see it as a passing toxic love interest.

We're both sure we're meant to be

there will come a time when we realize we must part

ways

it'll be a realization ridden with happiness

and it'll be the best day

Of my life.

Wishful Thinking

Pessimism scares me

binds me to ultimate failure

seals us together and berates my soul

toys with my entire being

and insists I will not win

because if there is no hope

if there is nothing left

then I will wither away

condemned to an eternity of drifting

this small truth

simply and definitively

is a possibility I will not entertain

a reality I shall not allow.

Keep Holding On

Some days I forget them

everyone I've lost to God

I forget the memories I once held near

this truth scares me

I find myself wishing

for easier things in life

because if I can forget you

lose grip of my past

am I not everything I feared and more?

Yet I remind myself

I have not thus far forgotten

these thoughts

are safe.

They are secure.

In this moment I do not fear

I am not forgetful

for these memories, I shall be infinitely grateful.

Marked Cars

We forget that people leave marks

much like places and thoughts

that old amusement park

those blue eyes that were somehow too dark

these bruises are left

but there is also a theft

everything you were before they found you

all of the things you once seemed bound to

they take pieces, filter them throughout the galaxies

leaving you to wonder

what you used to be

because these things they take are not so discreet

they're taking your history, rewriting it as their

victories

this will not go unanswered

you will cling to the dark eyes, the dark skies, and

the amusement parks

you will stand with your head held high

and remind these thieves that you are whatever you

wish to be

despite your warped history.

Guilty Conscience

I fear that I am irredeemable

these thoughts plague me

if I cannot atone for my perceived sins

does that not make me a lost cause

a drifter who cannot be saved?

I am guilty of much and it is a nightmare

a dream like state where I awake terrified

that one day the dream will end

and I will be faced with all of my wrongs

faced with a new reality

that irredeemable was the perfect word to describe me.

Holiday Trip

My manic days feel like a homecoming

A warm welcome from a family that I've been absent from

too long

it opens up to me like a flower to sunlight

and gathers me in its arms to shield me from the

harshness of reality

offers an extended stay at the vacation destination I call

Mania.

The feats I accomplish, the tasks I mark as complete

seem worth the inevitable exhaustion I know will befall me

because when my stay ends

and my welcome is rescinded

I will be forced to return to a mind free of whatever elixir which Mania supplies to me.

The return will not be warm, and it will not feel safe

I shall land in the world abruptly

thrust with a carelessness back into a place

that could only be known as depression

and await my inescapable invitation back home.

Bared Soul

I am occasionally happy

most often when I'm being useful

I am witty and I laugh a lot

because it distracts people

sometimes I'm selfish

I choose to wallow in my pain

though, I'm still generous

what's the point in giving anything

if you aren't offering everything?

I am resilient and determined

though would I be, had I not suffered?

Would I smile and laugh through my vices?

Would I have succumbed to a different reality

in which I had nothing but me to worry about?

I am who I am

and though it is scary, it is also freeing

I am me.

Used To Be

I was once translucent

willing to allow anyone

a glimpse into my life

I permitted the world to see my soul

and I did not fear what they might find.

That's who I used to be.

I willed the pieces

of my fractured mind

to flood the universe, welcomed all of the pain

and freely gave my soul to this place.

That's who I used to be.

Now transparency is terrifying

nudity under the watchful eye of the masses

induces indescribable fear in me.

I am no longer who I was.

Yet the person I was forced to be, she has

protected me.

Overwhelmed By Words

Emotions are much like a well written book

you don't quite know what you'll feel

when everything comes full circle

but you know the journey

has the potential to devastate you

how do you find the correct words

to offer correct representation

for such all-encompassing sentiments?

I search vehemently, and with heavy fervor

for an escape from this overwhelming reality of mine.

So that I may leave behind the inevitable devastation

the world is bound to grant me.

Your Arms

Your presence brings such pleasure in abundance-it

courts pain

a beautiful agony I yearn to capture, in vain

your arms provide a space in which I am content

a feeling I am not often lent

I vow to remain here forever if you shall have me

I cannot fathom a world in which

you would deny me.

Allow me an eternity here beside you

ensure me a millennium spent in happiness

as I lay in your arms dreading the passing of this.

Sleep Paralysis X Anxious Thoughts

I am trapped in my soul

with no control of my body

I breathe but I do not command my lungs

this life is a lucid dream

and I'm stuck beneath restraints made of steel

I am a statue

turned to stone by the eyes of the earth

I am paralyzed.

by fear and the truth, I am caught.

Inspiration

You are why I believe in the extraordinary

why I admire the commitment

in relentlessness.

Why I believe I can meet every goal I set.

You motivate me

to bypass the insecurities I have buried

you are dedicated to exceeding

I see you and acknowledge your need for healing

and I wish to tell you, wish for you to see

you are the reason

I've sworn to this deed

I'll be nothing short

of extraordinarily me.

Blackness

My skin is a weapon

of mass destruction

started wars and

tore down economies

my skin is a blessing

inspired thousands

and saved generations

my Blackness is fearsome

used to validate violence

my Blackness is a shield

from the darkness

of these truths, but also

the brightness of the sun

my soul is unique and scarred

my skin has picked my place in this world.

my Blackness is used to justify my plight.

I am scarred and beautiful, and Black. And I will fight

for my right to be that.

Chicago

I miss the silence of a busy, never sleeping city.

It offers a different quiet than the silence of

loneliness.

And in it, I find myself surrendering to the

emptiness of that sound.

Laying down my weapons of dissent and making this

place

my new home. '

Resilient

My trauma made me strong and brave

that's what they all say

the struggles I've faced in life

prepared me for society,

they try to convince me constantly.

But I didn't want to be strong

I most certainly did not want to be brave

I wanted to be saved.

Resiliency is something I'd rather

never had the misfortune of acquiring.

Yet this burden was given to me

so I'll wear it like armor

shield myself with great ardor

yet teach my future daughter

that she need not be strong

I'd much rather keep her safe

from anything that might go wrong.

I was here.

Everyone wants to be remembered

we all wish to stamp our name on this world

make it known that we occupied a space here

stand apart from the masses

and note our unique contributions to this universe.

I wish to do the same

but I have such a big soul and such a large voice

I worry that a stamp would not suffice.

I must leave my mark on this earthly plane

in a way that pays tribute to my true essence.

I will tag this world in great large letters

I shall make my signature a work of art.

And I will infuse my entire being

inside each word I write.

That will be my legacy.

Nice To See You Again

I am comfortable in my pain

home is where it hurts

where no feeling is in vain.

My ailments are familiar

they make sense to me

so does jumping from a pillar.

These thoughts provide solidarity

something I can cling to

yet within them a sense of polarity

I am lying atop a mountain

trying to grab onto a nearly tethered line

because I know within my soul

this pain is going to keep me safe.

It's a good friend of mine.

My choice, my body, my life.

I am mine.

My body belongs to me.

My life is mine to live.

My afterlife is mine to worry over.

My womb is mine to police.

My pregnancy is mine to terminate.

No one else's.

These choices are not up for grabs.

These decisions are not up to a vote.

These life altering events are mine.

No one else's.

I am not property.

I am not yours.

I am mine.

And. No. One. Else's.

Vacation

I miss being away

gone from the shackles

of my usual life and

the people forcing me to stay

I crave the ability to simply leave

and never return

I miss having an ocean

between me and

my incessant thoughts

I wish to be freed from the anguish

that lives in my reality

and vanquish the pain that it brings

I miss the naivety of being young

and believing that I could be happy

wherever I was in this world

having endless faith and never

wishing to let it all drift away.

I miss the possibility of taking a permanent

an everlasting and forever relaxing

irreversible extended stay.

I am older now and less naive

I cannot go on vacation

permanent of brief

because there is already so much

expected of me.

Impossible Questions

What do you want to be when you grow up?

I hated being asked that

as if I wasn't already drowning in this moment

as if I could possibly look past it

What do you want to give the world?

A question id never have an answer for

a question I'd burned to the ground in horror

What do you want to leave behind?

Brings out memories which aren't mine

I've been here before, I know this place

so I'll turn my soul into a song,

and pray that the pieces I leave behind

are vast enough to mark even space

I don't know the solution, don't know the words

can't give them what they want

cant sling together a few verbs.

I don't know what I want to be

I don't know what I want to give

but if I can't be remembered in this world

who the hell cares about any of it?

Revealing Me

Pasts are interesting

to know and understand

why a person is who they are

peel back the layers of charisma

which they've built to protect them from the world

seeing all that someone has suffered

and pinpointing the moment they decided

"I'll be the one to break the cycle"

it is, in my opinion, the most naked anyone can be.

When they reveal all they are to you

and there are no doors behind the curtain.

I aspire to bare myself to someone in that way

first I must address the trauma of my past

as I have not yet shown myself such nakedness.

They say that's the first step.

Ink of Me

Being in love with literature

is being in love with

the possibility of a way home

when I read a new story

I give myself over to the world

which spins delicately between each line

threads itself into each syllable

in each sentence I find

another escape route

I belong to the ink

of this story

I am the parchment used in the making

of different worlds.

For this gift I will forever be grateful.

I am in debt to the purveyors of these worlds.

And these words.

Growing Up

I wish I could age backwards

find a way to pack up

this baggage, that weighs on me

history might not repeat

if I could be allowed to protect myself

from the darkness which screams

I'd love to age backwards

begin anew, and remind myself of

all the wonderful things I might do.

A Future

I wish for a silence I can never obtain

a quiet inside of my brain

yet for sound to be nonexistent for me

I must come to terms and find peace

with these thoughts and images that badger me

silence isn't a possibility

not if I'm terrified of the simple idea of therapy.

How will I move past this fear

this sentiment that I will not be long for here

it's an impossibility which

would require me to be anything other than me.

And this is a task I am incapable of completing.

Opposite Of Progress

I've been stuck lately

almost suspended in time and waiting

for something extraordinary to happen

maybe it doesn't have to be extraordinary

anything to wake me from the slumber I'm in.

Because this dream-like state cannot be all I have to offer.

These cemented feet cannot be all I give to the world.

Yet I don't know how to wake up and just.

Move.

Good Man In A Storm

Life is difficult yet something we all wish to protect

sometimes we all want to disappear but

I fear for me, it is not time yet.

There are so many things to be done

so many people who have gone.

These tasks we must complete

because there's no one left to remind us to compete

against life when it badgers us

throws daggers at us and leaves us to bleed.

Yet we will continue and yield never

though life is difficult it is what we have now

and forever.

About the Author

Aariona Harris is currently studying English Literature full-time. She balances a full-time job and college while also finding time to write. Her passion is reading, especially classic literature. Writing provides her with a sense of belonging.

She has a passion for literature, just like other members of literary history. Her desire is to share this love with everyone.

Aariona has had her poetry published in various journals. This book is a product of a chaotic life. Every poem and word brought Aariona healing and acceptance.

Facebook:

Instagram

X: X

Thank you for reading these expressions.
Reviews are greatly appreciated.